TOP SPEEDS

HORSE — 75 KM (46 MILES) PER HOUR

ELECTRIC SKATEBOARD — 37KM (23 MILES) PER HOUR

DOG — 70 KM (43.5 MILES) PER HOUR

SPEEDBOAT — 511 KM (317.5 MILES) PER HOUR

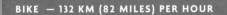

NOW THAT'S FAST!: SPEEDBOATS

RABBIT — 72 KM (45 MILES) PER HOUR

HUMAN — 45 KM (28 MILES) PER HOUR

BIKE — 132 KM (82 MILES) PER HOUR

NOW THAT'S FAST!
SPEEDBOATS

KATE RIGGS

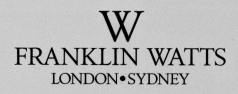

FRANKLIN WATTS
LONDON•SYDNEY

First published in the UK in 2011 by
Franklin Watts
338 Euston Road
London NW1 3BH

Franklin Watts Australia
Level 17/207 Kent Street
Sydney NSW 2000

First published by Creative Education,
an imprint of the Creative Company.
Copyright © 2010 Creative Education
International copyright reserved in all countries.
No part of this book may be reproduced in any
form without written permission from
the publisher.

ISBN 978 1 4451 0586 4
Dewey number: 623.8'231

A CIP catalogue record for this book
is available from the British Library.

Printed in China

Franklin Watts is a division of
Hachette Children's Books,
an Hachette UK company.
www.hachette.co.uk

Book and cover design by Blue Design
(www.bluedes.com)
Art direction by Rita Marshall

Photographs by Corbis (Patrick Bennett, Bettmann),
Dreamstime (Gvision, Sportslibrary), Getty
Images (PATRICK HERTZOG/AFP, Simeone Huber,
FRANCISCO LEONG/AFP, JEFF PACHOUD/AFP,
Piotr Powietrzynski, Quinn Rooney, Martin Rose/
Bongarts, Topical Press Agency), iStockphoto
(Arthur Achtelik)
Every atttempt has been made to clear copyright.
Should there be any inadvertent omission, please
contact the publisher for rectification.

A speedboat is a boat with a powerful **engine**. The engine makes the speedboat go fast through the water. Many speedboats can travel faster than 160 kilometres per hour (kph)!

A speedboat's engines push it through the water. The speedboat leaves a track behind it that is known as a wake.

engine

Speedboats are made of a strong material called fibreglass. They are usually long and narrow in shape, with a pointed front. This makes the speedboat more streamlined, so that it cuts faster through air and water.

8

A speedboat's sleek, streamlined shape helps it to slice through the water.

Speedboats are a great way to
have fun on the water.

People use speedboats to travel
fast over the water. Many people
just use speedboats to have fun,
but some speedboats are also used
for racing. People race speedboats
on rivers, lakes and the sea.

Speedboats called hydroplanes
(see page 16) are very light. They
skim over the surface of the water.

There are different types of racing speedboats. Bigger speedboats called go-fast boats have room for up to five passengers. But smaller speedboats carry only the driver.

The driver controls where the speedboat goes and how fast it travels. He or she sits in the **cockpit**. In some racing speedboats, strong metal bars called a roll cage hold the cockpit together and keep the driver safe.

Racing speedboats can be dangerous because of the high speeds, so drivers are well protected.

SPEEDBOATS

Hydroplanes are the smallest racing speedboats. They have two parts on the sides called sponsons, which are like an aeroplane's wings. Sponsons help the boat float on the water. A hydroplane can zoom across the water at speeds of over 320 kph!

The name 'hydroplane' combines a word for 'water' with the word 'plane'.

sponson

The first speedboat race was held in 1904 on a river in the state of New York, USA. The boat that won the race had a top speed of 40 kph. People thought that was really fast! But soon people made speedboats that went even faster.

This early speedboat from the 1930s was called the 'Empire Day'.

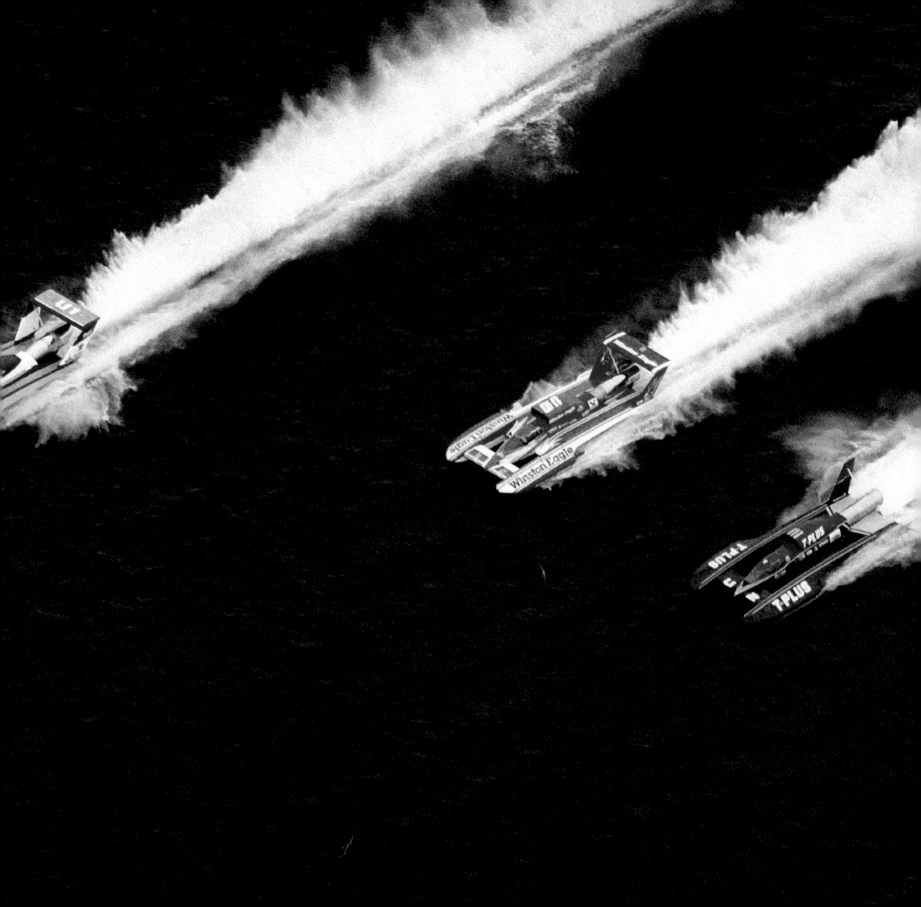

Speedboat racing is fast and furious. Drivers compete to be the fastest over a course of water with long straights and tight turns. Speedboat racing is dangerous, but recent changes, such as making drivers wear a harness, have made it safer.

On a tight race course, drivers steer very carefully to make sure that they do not collide with other speedboats.

21

Speedboat drivers like racing a fast boat. They hold on tightly to the steering wheel and race their boat to the finish!

Fast Facts

The current water speed record was set by Australian Ken Warby in 1978. He broke all records with an average speed of 511 kph. Amazingly, he built his boat himself in his back garden!

There are currently three teams aiming to beat the water speed record. These are the *American Challenge, Quicksilver* from the UK, and *Aussie Spirit* from Australia.

Speedboat racing is still one of the most dangerous sports in the world. Speedboat drivers now have to pass a lot of safety tests before they can race against other drivers.

Glossary

cockpit – the place where the driver sits in a speedboat or aeroplane

course – a set area of land or water over which a race is held

engine – a machine inside a vehicle that gives it the power to move

fibreglass – a strong, light material made of meshed glass fibres

harness – safety straps that attach someone or something to a vehicle

streamlined – a smooth shape that is designed to cut through air and water

Read More about It

Fast! Speedboats, Ian Graham,
QED Publishing, 2010

Website

Speedboat Colouring Page
http://www.coloring.com/color/speedboat
This page has a picture that can be coloured in online.

Index